The Simon and Schuster

# Picture Dictionary
# of Phonics
## from /ā/ to /zh/

The Simon and Schuster

# Picture Dictionary of Phonics
## from /ā/ to /zh/

by Linda Hayward

pictures by Carol Nicklaus
assisted by David Prebenna

A Little Simon Book
Published by Simon & Schuster, Inc., New York

Text copyright © 1984 by Linda Hayward
Illustrations copyright © 1984 by Carol Nicklaus
All rights reserved including the right of reproduction in whole or in
part in any form
Published by LITTLE SIMON, a division of Simon & Schuster, Inc.,
1230 Avenue of the Americas, New York, New York 10020.
Also available in Julian Messner library edition.
Printed in U.S.A.
10 9 8 7 6 5 4 3 2 1
LITTLE SIMON and colophon are registered
trademarks of Simon & Schuster, Inc.

ISBN 0-671-43102-1

For Danya – L.H.
For Eric, David, and Kate...and the mews – C.N.

/ā/

Rain delays the race eight days.

The /ă/ sound is the sound you hear
in the middle of the word **ran**.

Pat ran past a panda stacking cans on Jan's veranda.

/âr/

The b<u>ear</u> upst<u>air</u>s rep<u>air</u>s sp<u>are</u> ch<u>air</u>s.

The /är/ sound is the sound you hear
at the end of the word **jar**.

Marge parks Clark's car by a large jar.

/b/

Both beavers board a bus bound for Boise.

The /bəl/ sound is the sound you hear at the end of the word **table**.

Mabel was able to label each table.

# /bl/

The /bl/ sound is the sound you hear at the beginning of the word **blue**.

Blake unlocks a box of blue blocks.

The /br/ sound is the sound you hear
at the beginning of the word **brown**.

Brenda brought a brown umbrella.

# /ch/

The /ch/ sound is the sound you hear at the beginning of the word **chairs**.

The checked chairs Chuck chose are charming.

The /d/ sound is the sound you hear at the beginning of the word **dogs**.

/d/

A dozen dogs in dotted derbies dove off the dock at dawn.

# /dr/

The /dr/ sound is the sound you hear at the beginning of the word **draws**.

Drake draws Drew's drapes.

The /dw/ sound is the sound you hear at the beginning of the word **dwells**.

<u>Dw</u>ight <u>dw</u>ells in a bright shell.

/ē/

The /ē/ sound is the sound you hear at the beginning of the word **each**.

Each of these three seals feels sleepy.

The <u>/ĕ/ sound</u> is the sound you hear
in the middle of the word **red**.

Kent sent Ed red thread.

/ə/

The /ə/ sound is the sound you hear at the beginning of the word **above**.

Amanda is above a big abyss.

The /ər/ sound is the sound you hear at the end of the word **wat<u>er</u>**.

/ər/

Hect<u>or</u> waits for hott<u>er</u> wat<u>er</u>.

The /f/ sound is the sound you hear at the beginning of the word **fish**.

Fifi is fond of photographing fish.

The <u>/fl/ sound</u> is the sound you hear at the beginning of the word **floor**.

<u>Fl</u>amingoes adore <u>Fl</u>oyd's <u>fl</u>oor.

**/fr/**

The /fr/ sound is the sound you hear at the beginning of the word **frog**.

Fred's a friendly frog from Fresno.

The /g/ sound is the sound you hear at the beginning of the word **gate**.

/g/

The ghosts, seeing guests at the gate, were aghast.

/gəl/

In the ju**ngle**, a si**ngle** spa**ngle**d ba**ngle** da**ngle**d.

The /gl/ sound is the sound you hear
at the beginning of the word **glove**.

The glove Glen sews glows.

/gr/

The /gr/ sound is the sound you hear at the beginning of the word **green**.

Greg agreed to make a great big green cake.

The /gw/ sound is the sound you hear in the middle of the word **penguins**.

/gw/

Gwen spins penguins.

# /h/

The /h/ sound is the sound you hear at the beginning of the word **hats**.

Hundreds of hats hover in Hal's hall.

The /h<u>w</u>/ <u>sound</u> is the sound you hear
at the beginning of the word **w<u>h</u>eels**.

<u>Wh</u>arton <u>wh</u>irls his <u>wh</u>eels and <u>wh</u>istles a<u>wh</u>ile.

The /ī/ sound is the sound you hear at the end of the word **pie**.

Dwight drives right by Clive's pie.

The /ĭ/ sound is the sound you hear in the middle of the word **sіx**.

Six little fish swim in Tim's middle dish.

The /ĭj/ sound is the sound you hear at the end of the word **pack<u>age</u>**.

The cabb<u>age</u> in the pack<u>age</u> hid a mess<u>age</u>.

The /îr/ sound is the sound you hear
at the end of the word **here**.

H<u>ere</u> is a m<u>ere</u> sph<u>ere</u> n<u>ear</u> some qu<u>eer</u> g<u>ear</u>.

/j/

The /j/ sound is the sound you hear at the beginning of the word **jumped**.

Jane jumped over the gingerbread just ahead of George.

The /k/ sound is the sound you hear
at the beginning of the word **cats**.

/k/

A <u>c</u>ouple of <u>c</u>ats in <u>c</u>ali<u>c</u>o <u>c</u>aps <u>c</u>ame to <u>K</u>alamazoo.

# /kl/

Clyde's in the closet, clowning around.

The /kr/ sound is the sound you hear at the beginning of the word **crows**.

/kr/

Crows crossed the creek with crates of cranberries.

# /ks/

Ma<u>x</u> pa<u>ck</u>s si<u>x</u> so<u>ck</u>s in Ni<u>ck</u>'s bo<u>x</u>.

The /kw/ sound is the sound you hear at the beginning of the word **quilts**.

Quentin acquires quilts quite quickly.

The /l/ sound is the sound you hear
at the beginning of the word **look**.

Lola likes to look at letters.

The /lē/ sound is the sound you hear at the end of the word **on<u>ly</u>**.

On<u>ly</u> Ju<u>lie</u> plays the ukule<u>le</u>.

# /m/

Many mice meet in the morning mist.

The /n/ sound is the sound you hear
at the beginning and end of the word **nine**.

<u>N</u>a<u>n</u>ette <u>kn</u>ows <u>n</u>i<u>n</u>e <u>n</u>ewts, <u>n</u>o<u>n</u>e <u>n</u>amed <u>N</u>i<u>n</u>a.

/ng/

The /ng/ sound is the sound you hear at the end of the word lo**ng**.

Fa**ng** hu**ng** the wro**ng** thi**ng** on a lo**ng** stri**ng**.

The /ngk/ <u>sound</u> is the sound you hear
at the end of the word **pi<u>nk</u>**.

Mo<u>nk</u> and Ha<u>nk</u> thi<u>nk</u> the pi<u>nk</u> tru<u>nk</u> sa<u>nk</u>.

/ō/

The /ō/ sound is the sound you hear in the middle of the word **boat**.

Ole slowly rows Joe's boat.

The /ŏ/ sound is the sound you hear in the middle of the word **brought**.

Todd brought an odd pot.

/ô/

All Paul saw was a small claw.

The /ôr/ sound is the sound you hear
at the end of the word **more**.

/ôr/

Doris st<u>or</u>es m<u>or</u>e <u>oar</u>s than d<u>oor</u>s.

/oi/

The /oi/ sound is the sound you hear in the middle of the word **toys**.

Royce enjoys a choice of toys.

The /o͞o/ sound is the sound you hear in the middle of the word **mo͞ose**.

Two new blue shoes suit Lou's moose.

# /o͝o/

The /o͝o/ sound is the sound you hear in the middle of the word **foot**.

The wolf put his foot in the brook.

The /ou/ sound is the sound you hear at the end of the word **cow**.

/ou/

The br<u>ow</u>n c<u>ow</u> is s<u>ou</u>thb<u>ou</u>nd n<u>ow</u>.

/p/

A pair of pigs paper Peter's purple pantry.

The /pl/ sound is the sound you hear
at the beginning of the word **place**.

/pl/

A place with plaid plumbing is pleasant.

# /pr/

April's present disguise won a prize.

The /r/ sound is the sound you hear
at the beginning of the word **rabbits**.

/r/

Rhonda read the rhyme she wrote to a roomful of rabbits.

# /s/

Cecil saw someone with seven sons cycling to Sioux City.

The /sk/ sound is the sound you hear
at the beginning of the word **school**.

/sk/

Skip scatters scarves at school.

# /skr/

The /skr/ sound is the sound you hear at the beginning of the word **scrubs.**

Stevie scrubs TV screens.

The /skw/ sound is the sound you hear at the beginning of the word **square**.

The squirrels at the square dance squashed Lance.

# /sl/

The /sl/ sound is the sound you hear at the beginning of the word **slide**.

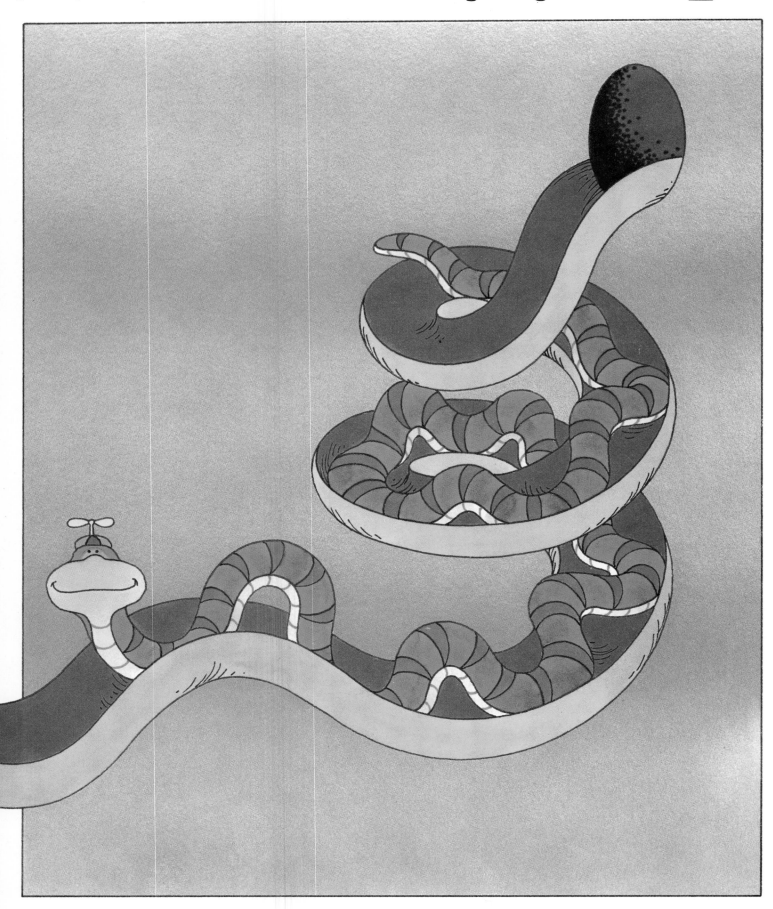

Clyde slowly slithered down the slide.

The /sm/ sound is the sound you hear at the beginning of the word **small**.

Jack walked SMACK! into a small smokestack.

# /sn/

The /sn/ sound is the sound you hear at the beginning of the word **snow**.

The trails of <u>sn</u>ails show in the <u>sn</u>ow.

The /sp/ sound is the sound you hear
at the beginning of the word **space**.

Spence finds a special place in outer space.

/spl/

The /spl/ sound is the sound you hear at the beginning of the word **splat**.

SPLAT! A splendid banana split ended.

The /spr/ sound is the sound you hear at the beginning of the word **spring**.

In the <u>spr</u>ing Bruce <u>spr</u>ays his <u>spr</u>uce.

The /st/ sound is the sound you hear
at the beginning of the word **stars**.

Stan stares at stars as he starts up the stairs.

The /str/ sound is the sound you hear at the beginning of the word **string**.

The <u>str</u>ange thing in the <u>str</u>eet is a <u>str</u>ing.

The /sw/ sound is the sound you hear at the beginning of the word **swing**.

SWISH! Swans swing swiftly.

The /sh/ sound is the sound you hear
at the beginning of the word **shoes**.

/sh/

Sheep shove shoes of all shapes down short chutes.

# /shən/

The /shən/ sound is the sound you hear at the end of the word **station**.

The cushion at the station is in motion.

The /shr/ sound is the sound you hear
at the beginning of the word **shrubs**.

/shr/

The <u>shr</u>ubs that flank Frank <u>shr</u>ank.

/t/

The /t/ sound is the sound you hear at the beginning of the word **ten**.

Ten tiny tasseled toads tiptoe into Tulsa.

The /tr/ sound is the sound you hear at the beginning of the word **tree**.

/tr/

Tracy's trombone is trapped in a tree.

The /tw/ sound is the sound you hear at the beginning of the word **twelve**.

The twins combine twelve balls of twine.

The /TH/ sound is the sound you hear at the beginning of the word **there**.

There is the feather that's unlike the others.

# /th/

The /th/ sound is the sound you hear at the beginning of the word **thing**.

The third thing Thelma found was thick and round.

The /thr/ sound is the sound you hear
at the beginning of the word **three**.

Three <u>thr</u>ushes flew <u>thr</u>ough the rushes.

/ŭ/

The /ŭ/ sound is the sound you hear at the beginning of the word **under**.

A number of ducks slumber under Huck's bunk.

The /ûr/ sound is the sound you hear in the middle of the word **bird**.

P<u>ear</u>l's b<u>ir</u>d s<u>ear</u>ches for a c<u>er</u>tain p<u>ur</u>ple c<u>ur</u>tain.

/v/

The /v/ sound is the sound you hear at the beginning of the word **vases**.

Various vases at Vivian's vanished.

The /w/ sound is the sound you hear at the beginning of the word **winter**.

<u>W</u>anda <u>w</u>elcomes <u>w</u>inter <u>w</u>eather.

/y/

For years Yolanda's had a yen for yellow yarn.

The /yoo̅/ sound is the sound you hear at the beginning of the word **uses**.

/yoo̅/

A few of the cubes Eunice uses are huge.

The /z/ sound is the sound you hear at the beginning of the word **zero**.

Zelda owns zero xylophones.

The /zh/ sound is the sound you hear
in the middle of the word **treasure**.

/zh/

Don's treasure is beyond measure.